W9-BEA-611

CHRISTMAS

Written by Alice K. Flanagan
Illustrated by Viki Woodworth

Content Adviser: Professor Sherry L. Field, Department of Social Science Education, College of Education, The University of Georgia

Reading Adviser: Dr. Linda D. Labbo, Department of Reading Education, College of Education, The University of Georgia

COMPASS POINT BOOKS

MINNEAPOLIS, MINNESOTA

Compass Point Books
3722 West 50th Street, #115
Minneapolis, MN 55410

Visit Compass Point Books on the Internet at *www.compasspointbooks.com*
or e-mail your request to *custserv@compasspointbooks.com*

Editors: E. Russell Primm and Emily J. Dolbear
Designer: The Design Lab

Library of Congress Cataloging-in-Publication Data

Flanagan, Alice K.
  Christmas / written by Alice K. Flanagan ; illustrated by Viki Woodworth.
    p. cm. — (Holidays and festivals)
  Includes bibliographical references and index.
  ISBN 0-7565-0085-0 (hardcover : lib. bdg.)
    1. Christmas—Juvenile literature. [1. Christmas. 2. Holidays.] I. Woodworth,
Viki, ill. II. Title. III. Series.
  GT4985.5 .F53 2002
  394.2663—dc21   2001001506

Table of Contents

See the reindeer bringing Santa Claus with gifts upon his sleigh. See the Christ child in a stable sleeping on a bed of hay.

Both these sights are part of the Christmas holiday. Most **Christians celebrate** Christmas on December 25. Christians believe Jesus Christ is the son of God. On this day, they remember the birth of Jesus Christ.

On December 25, people also celebrate the day Santa Claus comes. They give gifts and send cards to one another.

How Christmas Got Its Name

Christians were the first to call December 25 "Christmas." On that day, they held a service, or **mass**. They called the service *Christes Maesse*. That means "Christ's Mass."

Hundreds of years ago, there were many dates for Jesus's birthday. Then, in the fourth century, the Christian Church chose to celebrate his birth on December 25. They chose this day because it was close to a Roman **festival** called *Saturnalia*.

Saturnalia

The Romans celebrated Saturnalia from December 17 to December 24. During the festival, they honored Saturn. He was the Roman god of farming. Saturn was also the god of plenty. For one day of Saturnalia, the Romans honored the birth of the Sun.

Saturnalia marked the beginning of winter. It also marked the start of a new year. It was a joyful celebration, much like Christmas is today. People decorated their houses with lights and **evergreen** branches and berries. Wars stopped. People gave gifts to one another. They wished everyone happiness and good luck.

Christians did not believe in the Roman gods. But they wanted to keep some part of the Saturnalia celebration. So they gave it a new name—Christmas.

They celebrated Christmas the day after Saturnalia, on Dec-

ember 25. They celebrated it in a new way. Christians chose that day to celebrate the birth of Jesus Christ. Ever since then, they have been telling the story of his birth.

Jesus and the Christmas Story

The Christmas story began about 2,000 years ago in the town of Bethlehem. At that time, Christians believe God sent his son Jesus to Earth.

Jesus's parents were Jewish. His father was a carpenter named Joseph. His mother's name was Mary. Joseph and Mary lived in the town of Nazareth. The Roman ruler ordered everyone back to the town where they were born so they could be counted. So Joseph and Mary had to go to Bethlehem.

Mary was almost ready to give birth to Jesus. Every inn in Bethlehem was full. A kind man let Joseph and Mary stay in his stable with the animals. There, Jesus Christ was born.

A bright star shone above the stable. Three kings followed that star to Bethlehem. They found the Christ child in the stable. They gave him gifts.

Nearby, some **shepherds** saw **angels** in the field. The angels told them to come to the stable. The shepherds brought gifts too. Today, giving gifts is an important part of Christmas.

Giving Gifts

In the United States, people give gifts on Christmas Eve or Christmas Day. In other countries, people give presents on January 6. This is called the Twelfth Night of Christmas, or the Epiphany.

On this day, the three kings visited the Christ child. They gave him gifts. Now people give gifts to honor this event.

Some people give gifts on December 6. On this day in A.D. 345, Saint Nicholas of Myra died.

Nicholas was a clergyman. He lived in the town of Patara in what is now Turkey. He gave gifts to the poor. He also worked **miracles**. After Nicholas died, the Christian Church called him a saint. Saints are holy people who help others.

Over the years, Saint Nicholas Day and Christmas became one holiday. Saint Nicholas (Saint Nick, for short) became the **patron saint** of Christmas.

In Holland, Saint Nicholas comes with a helper. His name is Black Peter, or *Bellsnickle*. He brings gifts to children who have been good. Black Peter scares the children who have been bad.

In Belgium, Saint Nicholas is called *Père Noël*. He visits houses twice. On December 4, he comes to find out which children have been good during the year. He returns on December 6 to bring them candy left in shoes and toys. The children who have been bad get sticks.

Who Is Santa Claus?

Some people believe that Dutch settlers brought the idea of Santa Claus to America in the 1600s. They called him *Sinterklass* (Saint Nicholas). Americans thought the name sounded like "Santa Claus." That's how Santa Claus got his name.

No one knew for sure what Santa Claus looked like. Some said he was tall and wore a beard. They said he dressed in churchman's clothing. Others thought of him as a jolly old elf.

No one knew how Santa brought his presents from house to house. Some people thought he rode a horse or a moose. Others said he used giant turkeys or reindeer to pull his sleigh.

In 1822, an American named Clement Moore wrote a poem about Saint Nick. It was called "A Visit from Saint Nicholas."

In the poem, Saint Nicholas drove a sleigh pulled through the sky

by eight reindeer. Saint Nicholas landed the sleigh on roofs. Then he slid down chimneys with a sack full of toys. The poem was published in a newspaper. The poem is still popular today.

In 1863, an American artist named Thomas Nast drew Santa Claus as a plump, jolly old man. He wore a red suit and had a white beard. This is the way most people picture Santa Claus today.

Two Holidays in One

On Christmas, many people celebrate two holidays. Christians go to church to celebrate the birthday of Jesus Christ. They also celebrate the arrival of Santa Claus.

Families share a special Christmas dinner. Then they gather around a brightly decorated Christmas tree. They give presents to one another. Many families sing old Christmas songs called carols.

In some countries, Christmas is a more religious holiday. In Mexico, the Christian celebration is called *Las Posadas*. People take part in a play about Mary and Joseph's trip to Bethlehem. The play lasts nine days. Then people have a party.

Mexicans hang a cardboard and papier-mâché pot called a *piñata*

from the ceiling. It is full of candy and toys. Children cover their eyes with a piece of cloth. Then they try to break the piñata with a stick.

In Spain, good children receive gifts from the three kings. In Italy, a fairy queen named La Befana brings gifts to the good children. People say the three kings visited La Befana on their way to see the Christ child.

Things You Might See on Christmas Day

The Christmas Crib

At Christmas, many Christians set up a **manger** scene in their homes. In the manger are tiny figures of Jesus, Mary, and Joseph. They are in the stable as they were on the first Christmas in Bethlehem.

A long time ago, farm animals were kept in stables. They ate food from open wooden boxes called mangers. When Jesus Christ was born, he had no bed so he was put in a manger.

Saint Francis of Assisi made the first manger scene. He lived in Italy in the early thirteenth century. He used real animals and real people. Over the years, the practice of putting up mangers spread to other parts of the world.

The Christmas Tree

Decorating a tree began in Germany during the 1500s. It spread to other countries in Europe and then the United States.

Today, the tree is an important part of Christmas around the world. It is not always an evergreen tree.

In India, children decorate mango or banana trees. In Africa, they put bells on palm trees. In China, people cut out paper lights, butterflies, and flowers. They hang them on trees outside their homes.

Santa Claus

Many countries have a character like Santa Claus. He brings children gifts. In Austria, they call him the Christkind (Christ child). Some call him Kris Kringle.

In France, he is called Père Noël (Father Christmas). In Poland, he is called Saint Nicholas. In Norway, he is called Jule Nissen. In Brazil, he is called Vovo Indo (Grandpapa Indian). In Japan, he is called Hoteiosho. In China, he is called Dun Che Lao Ren (Christmas Old Man).

The Russians have a woman Santa Claus. She is called Babouschka (grandmother).

Christmas Stockings

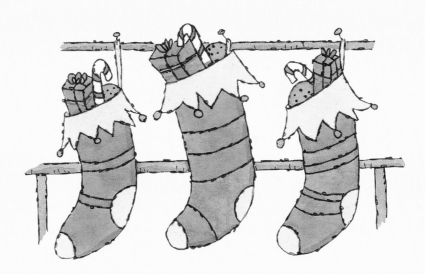

A long time ago, Saint Nicholas wanted to give gold to a poor man and his three daughters. However, he did not want the family to know who was giving the gift. So he threw three small bags of gold down their chimney. One of the bags fell into a stocking hanging by the fire to dry.

Ever since, children hang up stockings the night before Christmas. In Belgium and France, children put out shoes instead of stockings.

The Poinsettia

The pretty red flowers you see at Christmas are called poinsettias. The poinsettia is named for Joel R. Poinsett. He brought the plant to the United States from Mexico in the 1800s. In Mexico, they call it the "Flower of the Holy Night." There is a story about the poinsettia.

A long time ago, a little girl was on her way to see the Christmas manger at church. She had no gift to bring to the Christ child. So, she picked some branches from a bush growing by the road. When she placed the branches next to the manger, the green leaves turned bright red. Ever since, the poinsettia is the Christmas flower.

What You Can Do on Christmas Day

Christmas is one of the busiest holidays. Most people are busy buying gifts and decorating their houses.

It is easy to forget how people celebrated the holiday long ago. They rested and did not work. They stopped fighting. They wished everyone peace and goodwill. They celebrated the coming of a new year.

Today, people can celebrate in the same way. Here are some ideas:

* Be a peacemaker at school, at home, and in your neighborhood.
* Forgive people who have hurt you.
* Be joyful. Cheer up those who are sad.
* Do something kind for a neighbor or friend.
* Give your time to an organization that helps the needy.

Glossary

angels messengers of God

celebrate to have a party or to honor a special event

Christians people who believe Jesus Christ is the son of God

evergreen a plant whose leaves or needles stay green all year round

festival a holiday or celebration

manger an open wooden box that holds food for farm animals

mass a church service

miracles events that cannot be explained

patron saint a holy person who helps others

shepherds people who take care of sheep

sleigh a sled pulled by horses or other animals

stable a building where farm animals are kept

Where You Can Learn More about Christmas

At the Library

Chris, Teresa. *The Story of Santa Claus.* London: Apple Press, 1992.

Hintz, Martin, and Kate Hintz. *Christmas: Why We Celebrate It the Way We Do.* Mankato, Minn.: Capstone Press, 1996.

Ouwendijk, George. *Santas of the World.* Bromall, Penn.: Chelsea House Publishers, 1998.

Restad, Penne L. *Christmas in America: A History.* New York: Oxford University Press, 1995.

On the Web

CHRISTMAS ON THE WEB: *http://www.holidays.net/christmas/*

For the story of Christmas, Christmas recipes, and holiday games

WORLDVIEW CHRISTMAS: *http://christmas.com/worldview/*

For a clickable map with information about Christmas celebrations around the world

THE WORLDWIDE HOLIDAY AND FESTIVAL SITE: *http://www.holidayfestival.com/*

For information about holidays and festivals around the world

Index

About the Author and Illustrator

Alice K. Flanagan writes books for children and teachers. Since she was a young girl, she has enjoyed writing. She has written more than seventy books. Some of her books include biographies of U.S. presidents and their wives, biographies of people working in our neighborhoods, phonics books for beginning readers, and informational books about birds and Native Americans. Alice K. Flanagan lives in Chicago, Illinois.

Viki Woodworth has illustrated and written numerous books for children. She lives with her husband and two teenage daughters in Seattle, Washington.